God's Will for my Body

Guidance for Adolescents

John Coblentz

Illustrated by Charity Riehl

CHRISTIAN LIGHT
PUBLICATIONS

Christian Family Living Series

Christian Family Living
This basic book of the series offers practical Scriptural help ranging from training toddlers to caring for aging parents. Each chapter closes with questions for further thought and action.

God's Will for My Body—Guidance for Adolescents
A workbook to help parents in teaching their children about adolescent changes.

God's Will for Love in Marriage—Cultivating Marital Intimacy
A study for engaged persons or married couples, offering practical, Biblical guidance for healthy intimacy in marriage. Includes a frank, Biblical approach to the controversial subject of family planning.

Courtship That Glorifies God—A Biblical Approach to Dating and Engagement
A reprint of Chapter 3 in *Christian Family Living.* Available as a booklet for study in youth groups, Bible schools, high schools, etc.

Singlehood That Glorifies God—Living With Eternal Purpose
A reprint of Chapter 4 in *Christian Family Living.* This booklet is for single people as well as for those willing to understand and respect single people.

What the Bible Says About Marriage, Divorce, and Remarriage
A Biblical approach to a battered subject, this study follows a question-and-answer format in showing what the Bible says and in offering practical help for resolving difficult situations.

Looking at Myself Before Loving Someone Else
A workbook to prepare young people for godly courtship.

Before You Say Your Vows
This premarital counseling guide for couples and counselors applies Biblical principles that govern closeness, communication, and lifelong commitment.

GOD'S WILL FOR MY BODY
Christian Light Publications
Harrisonburg, Virginia 22802

First edition 1992. Second edition 2019.
Printed in the United States of America

ISBN: 978-0-87813-542-4

First printing, 2019

Cover and Interior Design: Elizabeth McMurray
Cover Graphics: Darin Vance, Getty Images

Table of Contents

Growing up has always had its bumps and scrapes and secret fears. God has given parents the weighty responsibility of helping their children become adults—safely. Sometimes that responsibility seems overwhelming. Other times it seems impossible. Besides the "normal" difficulties children face growing up, today a host of degrading influences threaten our young people.

This workbook is not intended to replace the responsibility of parents, but to provide help. The material is not intended for indiscriminate reading by children or young people. Nor is it designed to be turned over to a young person at the opportune age as an assignment. The best way to use this workbook is for parent and child to work through it together, the parent reviewing the lesson first and then guiding the child.

No age can be set as the ideal age for a young person to learn the material in this workbook. Changes occur at different ages for different young people. Situations and need can vary greatly. It is wise, however, for young people to be aware of the changes puberty brings before they experience them. Ideally they should learn these things from their parents first, rather than from other sources.

Some parents may choose to take their young people through this workbook from beginning to end. Others may want to use only certain parts and teach the remainder as parent-to-child instruction. Or, some parents may cover certain lessons at one age and wait until later to discuss other lessons. Due to the sensitive nature of the information, parents should be careful with what is done with this workbook while it is being used and when it is completed. Filing the workbook may avoid the embarrassment of younger children or visiting children picking it up.

Both the child and the parent should be involved in the workbook. The child, for example, might read the Scriptures and the exercises, and the parent read the instructional sections. Parents, of course, may arrange this as is suitable for their situation. The Scriptures in the workbook provide opportunities for the parent to lead in further discussion and explanation. Numerous other places provide opportunities to stop and discuss ideas, make applications, and give personal illustrations. A child readily warms to a parent who shares appropriate experiences from his own growing up—blunders, nervousness, fears, and misunderstandings.

In some cases it may be suitable for both parents to be involved, but likely a father will work with his son and a mother with her daughter. At times the activities are divided according to the gender of the child.

Because the subject matter of this workbook is not household talk, it provides opportunities to teach discretion. Some subjects are right and good in their place but are not suitable for general discussion. Parents, keep a relaxed and open atmosphere in discussing these lessons with your child. But practice and teach reserve in discussing such issues as male and female differences and private body organs and functions. If parents of the past are to be blamed for being too hush-hush in these matters, they are at least to be praised for knowing there is a place for hush. Society today has wrought more evil by its indiscriminate talking about sex than the past ever did by its excessive reserve.

We trust this workbook will help to maintain the Biblical perspective—gladly accepting the reality of our physical bodies and their functions, but showing reserve, modesty, and dignity in the way we discuss such things and conduct ourselves.

Note about Lessons 9 and 10: As society seems to go further and further from God and people live ever more selfishly and sinfully, issues become common that were not common in the past. Godly parents should discuss such issues with their young people. Lessons 9 and 10 deal with two of these: gender confusion and the use of technology. Look over these lessons before your child begins; you may want to discuss parts of them with your child or give him or her some directions before doing the work.

—John Coblentz

God Made My Body

Lesson 1

God, My Creator

"The Lord God formed man of the dust of the ground, and breathed into his nostrils the breath of life; and man became a living soul" (Genesis 2:7).

"Thou hast covered me in my mother's womb. I will praise thee; for I am fearfully and wonderfully made: marvellous are thy works; and that my soul knoweth right well. My substance was not hid from thee, when I was made in secret, and curiously wrought in the lowest parts of the earth. Thine eyes did see my substance, yet being unperfect; and in thy book all my members were written, which in continuance were fashioned, when as yet there was none of them" (Psalm 139:13-16).

"And God saw every thing that he had made, and, behold, it was very good" (Genesis 1:31).

Answer these questions.

1. Who made our bodies? ____________________

2. What did God say about everything He made? ______________________________

3. What are three words the psalmist uses to describe how he is made?

______________ ______________ ______________

4. Is your body good or bad? ______________

God is the Creator of all things and all people. God made you. The psalmist says God was planning all your body parts even while you were being formed inside your mother, before you were complete.

Today, scientists know your body cells contain a "code" called DNA. This tremendously complex code is part of every cell in your body. It contains the formula for your body—it determines how tall you will be, the color of your eyes and hair, the length of your limbs, and the makeup and function of all your organs.

Some scientists do not believe in God. They say our bodies evolved, that we changed little by little from simple creatures into complex human beings. But even the most "simple" creatures have a very complex cell structure.

From the Bible, we know God is the Creator of all things and all people. Knowing this helps us to understand how we are to use our bodies.

Read Psalm 100 and complete the activities.

5. Who made us, according to verse 3? ______________

6. Who did not make us (same verse)? ______________

7. What does verse 5 say about the Lord? ______________

____

8. What does each of these verses say about our response to God?
   - **a.** Verse 2: We should ______________ the Lord.
   - **b.** Verse 4: We should ______________ and ______________ the Lord.

Read Romans 12:1 and fill in the blanks.

9. "I beseech you therefore, brethren, by the ________________ of God, that ye present your ________________ a living sacrifice, ________________, acceptable unto God, which is your reasonable ________________."

Fill in the blanks.

10. I am _______ feet _______ inches tall. My eyes are ________________ (color), and my hair is ________________. My build, the shape of my nose and ears, and all my body parts inside and out were designed by ________________. In my cells, God put a special code called ________________ to determine the size, shape, and functions of my body. After God had created all things, He said it was very ________________. God wants me to ________________ Him with my body and to ________________ Him for being such a wise and wonderful Creator.

Do this activity.

11. God controls many things about you, but He also gives you the responsibility of making right choices. He made your body, but you choose how you take care of it and how you use it. Beside each of the things below, write *God* if it is controlled by God, and write your name if you have the responsibility of making those choices.

____________ height

____________ hair color

____________ length of arms

____________ intelligence

____________ skin color

____________ color of eyes

____________ size of hands & feet

____________ shape of nose & ears

____________ weight

____________ clothing

____________ hair length & cleanliness

____________ education & training

____________ muscle tone

____________ lifework

____________ personal salvation

____________ habits

Look at the list on the left. These are things you did not choose. God gave them to you, and your best response is, "Thank You, Lord." Now look at the list on the right. These are things that require right choices on your part. Your best response is, "Lord, I want to do Your will." Below, you can read each prayer and sign your name to let God know this is how you feel.

Prayer

Lord, You made me. My body is a wonderful creation and shows how wise You are. I know I can trust Your "code" for how my body grows and develops. I thank You for making me, and I accept my body as a wonderful gift.

(Signed) ____________________

Lord, there are so many things I can do with my body—right and wrong. But because You made me, I want to do what pleases You. Help me to be wise in all my choices. I want to take care of my body and use it to serve You all my life.

(Signed) ____________________

Commitment

Parents need to make right choices too. They are responsible to give good instruction and helpful advice as their children grow into adulthood. Then their children can teach their own children, and each generation is taught to serve the Lord. The following paragraph is for parents to fill out.

Dear ____________________,

I thank God for you. God has placed you into our family, and I am grateful to Him for you. I love you just as you are, but I know you will grow and change. As you grow, I want to teach you more about your body and God's will for you so you can make wise choices in life. As we work and play and worship together, I will instruct you. When you have questions, don't be afraid to ask. I will do my best to answer your questions, because I am committed to you.

(Signed) ____________________

God Made Male and Female Bodies

Lesson 2

Male and Female Are Part of God's Plan

"So God created man in his own image, in the image of God created he him; male and female created he them" (Genesis 1:27).

"The Lord God said, It is not good that the man should be alone; I will make him an help meet [suitable] for him" (Genesis 2:18).

God's Plan Is Good

Can you imagine what the world would be like with only men in it? Or how about only women? God knew such a world would not be suitable. He planned for both male and female people.

Even with babies and children there are differences in male and female. But the differences become greater as children grow into adults. These differences are part of God's creation. Like all the rest of His creation, they are good. We can thank God not only for giving us bodies, but also for giving us male and female bodies. This is part of God's wise plan.

God made male bodies different in some ways from female bodies. A man's body usually is bigger than a woman's body. Men usually have broader shoulders and stronger limbs. God made men this way because God intended that in a family the man would provide for his wife and be her leader and protector.

A woman's body is usually smaller than a man's body. Her body is not as suited to rugged work, but it is just right for the work God has given to her. In a home, a woman looks after the family's needs, making meals and caring for children. A woman's softer voice and gentler touch can make a home rich with security and love.

God wants men to be loving leaders. He wants them to be considerate of the needs of women. He wants men not only to be strong physically, but to be strong spiritually. He wants men to follow Him, to do what is right even when others do wrong, and to lead their families in God's way. Men who fearlessly live for God and lovingly lead their families are pleasing to God. They are God's men.

God wants women to be gentle and supportive. He wants them to honor their husbands, not boss them. He wants women to be godly in their hearts and to train children to be respectful, obedient, and kind. Women who are godly, who support their husbands, and who patiently mother their children are pleasing to God. They are God's women.

Men need the gentleness of women, and women need the strength of men. God made male and female this way. We can thank God for the differences in men and women, because working together, they can build happy families and godly homes.

Fill in the blanks.

1. "The LORD God said, It is not ________________ that the man should be ________________; I will make him an help ________________ for him" (Genesis 2:18).

2. All people are either ________________ or ________________.

3. A man's body is usually ________________ than a woman's body.

4. Men usually have broader ________________ and stronger ________________.

5. A woman's softer ________________ and gentler ________________ can make a home rich with security and love.

6. We should thank God for the differences in ________________ and ________________, because working together, they can build happy ________________ and ________________ homes.

Underline the proper choice.

7. I am a (male, female).
8. When I grow up, I will be a (man, woman).
9. I should be (happy, dissatisfied) with the way God made me.
10. When I am grown up, God wants me to be (godly, unloving).

Answer these questions.

11. Do all strong men follow God? ________________
12. Who was a very strong man in the Old Testament? (See Judges 14:5, 6.)

    ____
13. Where did this strong man end up? (See Judges 16:21, 30.) ________________
14. What kind of strength does God want young men to have? (See 1 John 2:14.) ________________
15. What makes a woman valuable to her husband? (See Proverbs 31:10.)

    ____
16. What makes her beautiful to God? (See Proverbs 31:30.) ________________
17. What did Jezebel do to her husband? (See 1 Kings 21:25.) ________________
18. How did Jezebel try to make herself beautiful? (See 2 Kings 9:30.)

    ________________ ________________

Getting a Right Start

What do you think is important for becoming God's men and God's women when we are grown up? We need to follow God's ways when we are young, right? The Bible says, "Train up a child in the way he should go: and when he is old, he will not depart from it" (Proverbs 22:6). That is why your parents have provided this workbook for you. They want you to walk in God's ways both now and when you are grown. Have you ever thanked God for your parents? Have you ever told your parents thank you for the training they are giving you? How about doing that now?

Dear God,

Thank You for my parents. Thank You for my mother. Thank You that You made her a woman. Thank You that You made my father a man. Please help them to be godly so they can teach me to be the godly person You want me to be.

(Signed) ____________________

Fill in *Mom* or *Dad* (or whatever you call your parents) in this thank you.

Dear ____________________,

Thank you for being my parent. Thank you for all the things you have done for me. Thank you for wanting to train me to be a godly (man, woman) when I grow up. I want to learn from you how to live for God. I love you.

(Signed) ____________________

Commitment

Fill in your child's name in this commitment.

Dear ____________________,

I am so glad God made you a (boy, girl). I know He wants you to grow up to be a godly (man, woman). I am committed to teaching and training you in God's ways, and I will do my best to live a life that you can follow. I thank God that you are my child. I love you.

(Signed) ____________________

When Boys Become Men

Lesson 3

Strong Young Men

"The glory of young men is their strength" (Proverbs 20:29).

"I have written unto you, young men, because ye are strong, and the word of God abideth in you, and ye have overcome the wicked one" (1 John 2:14).

In the last lesson, we saw how men usually have stronger bodies than women. Boys like strength. They look forward to becoming strong men. The Bible describes strength in several ways.

Some men in the Bible were strong physically. Samson killed a lion with his bare hands. One night he wanted to leave town, but his enemies had locked the gate. He tore the gate—bars, pins, and all—out of the city wall and carried it to the top of a hill. Benaiah, one of David's men, fought a huge Egyptian. The Egyptian had a spear like a "weaver's beam," and Benaiah had only a club. But Benaiah managed to knock the Egyptian's spear out of his hand and used the Egyptian's own spear to kill him. Goliath was a strong man. He was nearly ten feet tall and wore armor that weighed more than most men.

But there is another kind of strength spoken of in the Bible. It is the strength that makes young men able do what is right. Daniel had this strength. He wouldn't eat food God had forbidden to the Jews, even though the king of Babylon had commanded this. Daniel's three friends refused to bow to an image, even though everyone around them was bowing and the king was threatening to throw them into a fiery furnace. Now that's strength!

In this lesson you will learn about some of the changes God planned in a boy's body for turning him into a man. Not all boys will become big and strong physically, but all who follow God can have the strength of Daniel and his three friends.

Which kind of strength do we need for each of the following? Write *P* for physical strength and *S* for spiritual strength.

1. ________ When I need to lift a bale of hay.

2. ________ When I am tempted to look at bad magazines.

3. ________ When my friends laugh at a dirty story.

4. ________ When my dad and I need to move a piece of furniture.

5. ________ When I need to do an errand quickly for my parents.

6. ________ When I am with people who are making fun of a handicapped person.

7. ________ When I am asked to carry a heavy pail of garbage outside.

Male Changes

> *"I will praise thee; for I am fearfully and wonderfully made" (Psalm 139:14).*
>
> *"If any man's seed of copulation go out from him, then he shall wash all his flesh in water" (Leviticus 15:16).*

Some of the things we will discuss here are things we do not talk about in normal conversation. This is not because we are ashamed of how God made us, but because some parts of our bodies are private. Remember, God made us, and everything God made is good. God wants us to be discreet, however, in the way we talk about our bodies.

Around the ages of 12 to 14, boys go through changes in their bodies. God made a special gland in the brain called the pituitary (pə tü′ ə ter′ e) gland. At the right time, this gland starts sending messages to other glands, telling them to start changes that will turn the boy into a man.

A boy will often have a growth spurt. He may grow several inches or more in one year. Sometimes there is an early growth spurt and a later one. Muscles begin to show more clearly. Usually the adolescent boy develops a hearty appetite, eating as much as or more than a grown man.

Other changes take place as well. The voice begins to deepen. Sometimes it becomes rather harsh or crackly for a time. Many boys experience the frustration of sudden changes in voice pitch, out of the deeper sound (which they like) into an embarrassing falsetto. Because of this, some boys don't like to talk much in group settings.

Male hormones also cause hair to begin to grow in various places—on the chin and upper lip, under the arms, and in the pubic area. Hair on the arms and legs also grows longer and thicker. Most boys are as pleased the first time they shave as they were the first time they were told they could mow the lawn. However, the novelty of shaving whiskers, like the novelty of mowing grass, soon wears off.

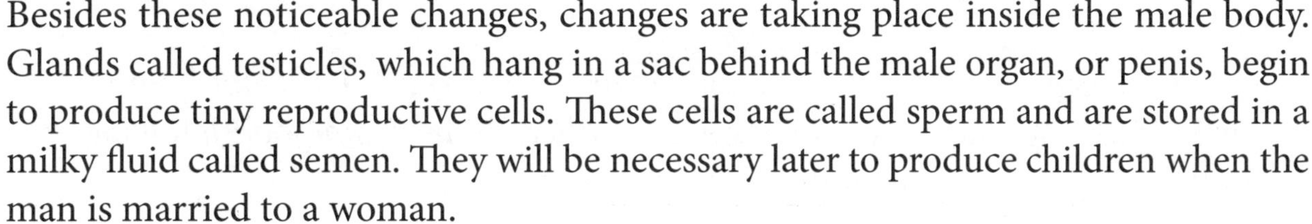

Besides these noticeable changes, changes are taking place inside the male body. Glands called testicles, which hang in a sac behind the male organ, or penis, begin to produce tiny reproductive cells. These cells are called sperm and are stored in a milky fluid called semen. They will be necessary later to produce children when the man is married to a woman.

During adolescence, from time to time the storehouse of sperm becomes full. The body may empty this extra semen through the penis. This usually takes place during the night. Often the boy has a dream at the same time. So these occurrences are sometimes called "wet dreams." If boys do not know what is happening, they may think something is wrong with them. Some boys think they have sinned. Neither is true. The body is simply relieving itself in a very proper and natural way.

During a wet dream the boy's penis may grow larger and become rigid. This is called erection. It does not happen only during a wet dream, but it may occur at other times too. Although erection is the body's natural response to stimulation, a boy may experience it without realizing why. This is normal. Some boys, however, try to stimulate erection by touching themselves because there is a pleasant feeling with erection. This is wrong. The best thing for a boy to do when he experiences erection during the day is to get busy doing something else.

When a boy has a wet dream, he should change his underclothes and wash himself. This does not mean semen is "germy." Washing is simply a good practice in cleanliness, just as we normally change and wash when we spill something on our clothes.

All these changes in a boy's body are part of God's plan for bringing him to manhood. Every boy should have the privilege of talking honestly and openly with his father about these changes in his body. Or if his father is not available, he should talk to another Christian adult man, such as his minister.

Discuss these questions with your parents.

8. Have you had fears that something was wrong with your body?

9. As a boy, have you experienced any physical changes described here?

10. As you develop physically, would you like to have occasional talks to discuss your questions and feelings?

A Special Warning

"But fornication, and all uncleanness, or covetousness, let it not be once named among you, as becometh saints; neither filthiness, nor foolish talking, nor jesting, which are not convenient: but rather giving of thanks" (Ephesians 5:3, 4).

"Whoso shall offend one of these little ones which believe in me, it were better for him that a millstone were hanged about his neck, and that he were drowned in the depth of the sea" (Matthew 18:6).

Boys and men who do not know the Lord sometimes think it is smart and fun to joke and tell dirty stories about their bodies and about sinful activities between men and women. This is "foolish talking" according to

God. It is making dirty something God intended to be pure and clean in its right place. When people begin to talk this way about their bodies, they soon are doing wrong things. Their minds become more and more impure.

Some young boys first learn about sex and changes in their bodies through older boys or men who are dirty and coarse in their speech. For the young boy, this can be the first step away from a right understanding. Now who is responsible for leading him astray? Jesus warned strongly against causing those who believe in Him to fall into sin.

The information you learn in this workbook is for you to discuss with your parents. It is not impure. It is part of God's plan for the development of your body. Discuss it freely and openly with your parents. But never take it and make jokes about it in an attempt to be smart or funny. There's nothing smart or funny about receiving God's anger, and there's nothing smart or funny about getting drowned in the depths of the sea!

Consider the following situations. Discuss with your parents first what you think Samson might have done, then what Daniel might have done, and finally what you should do.

11. You are in a group where a dirty story is told. Everyone laughs, and they look at you expecting you to laugh too.

12. Someone shows you a dirty magazine and wants you to look at the pictures.

13. Some boys whistle at girls, and they wave back. The boys ask you to go with them to talk to the girls.

A Prayer for Boys

Dear God,

Thank You for making me male. Thank You for Your plan for my body. Keep me from foolish and dirty language. I want to be pure and a good example for those who are younger. Help me never to cause others to sin. Help me to have the kind of strength Daniel had so that when I am tempted, I will do what is right. Amen.

(Signed) ____________________

When Girls Become Women

Lesson 4

Beautiful Women

"Who can find a virtuous woman? for her price is far above rubies" (Proverbs 31:10).

"O thou fairest among women . . . Behold, thou art fair, my beloved, yea, pleasant" (Song of Solomon 1:8, 16).

"If a woman have long hair, it is a glory to her" (1 Corinthians 11:15).

Just as men enjoy being strong, so women enjoy being beautiful. Girls do not look forward to having muscular bodies as boys do. Their natural desire instead is to be beautiful. Their hair, according to God's direction, is to be left uncut. A woman's long flowing hair is "a glory to her." It is part of her beauty given by God.

Of course, God wants a woman to be beautiful in her heart. This is the real beauty of a godly woman. A woman with a beautiful appearance and a foolish heart is a poor combination. God's Word says, "As a jewel of gold in a swine's snout, so is a fair woman which is without discretion" (Proverbs 11:22).

Furthermore, this does not mean women are to show their beauty to everyone. Although God made women physically beautiful, He says a woman is to veil her head and cover her body. The beauty of a woman is for her husband to enjoy in private, not for her to display in public. We will look at this more in a later lesson.

In this lesson we will look at some of the changes that take place in a girl's body to make her a woman. These are changes God designed for a woman's beauty and attractiveness. They are good. But these changes also mean that a girl must become more discreet and modest in her appearance and actions. This is not because she is ashamed of her body, but because her physical beauty is not for public display.

Answer these questions.

1. Where is a woman's most important beauty? ____________________
2. Do you know a beautiful woman who is not very attractive physically? __________
3. What makes her beautiful? ____
4. When a woman shows her physical beauty in public, do you think this will make her marriage stronger or weaker? ____________________ Discuss why this is so.

Many women are tempted to try to add to their physical beauty and neglect the beauty of their hearts. Read the following verses and list in the first column what makes a woman's hearts beautiful. In the second column list what a woman should not use to make herself beautiful.

Verse	True Beauty	Artificial Beauty
1 Timothy 2:9, 10	____________ ____________ ____________	____________ ____________ ____________ ____________
Titus 2:4, 5	____________ ____________ ____________ ____________ ____________ ____________ ____________	
1 Peter 3:3, 4	____________ ____________ ____________	____________ ____________ ____________

"We have a little sister, and she hath no breasts" (Song of Solomon 8:8).

"If a woman have an issue, and her issue in her flesh be blood, she shall be put apart seven days" (Leviticus 15:19).

Unlike a boy, a girl experiences very little change in her voice. But like a boy, a girl usually has growth spurts. Often a girl's rapid growth occurs before boys of the same age, so that a ten- or twelve-year-old girl may appear to be older than ten- or twelve-year-old boys. Girls usually don't mind this, but for boys it may be quite a different story. A boy who finds his younger sister taller than he may well begin piling the mashed potatoes higher.

The same gland that changes boys into men—the pituitary gland—works in the girl's body to change her into a woman. It begins sending messages to different parts of the body. A changing girl begins to grow hair under the arms and in the pubic area. At the same time, she finds her breasts beginning to grow larger. This may bring a measure of self-consciousness to a girl, but it also gives her a deepening sense of becoming a woman. Most girls view it positively.

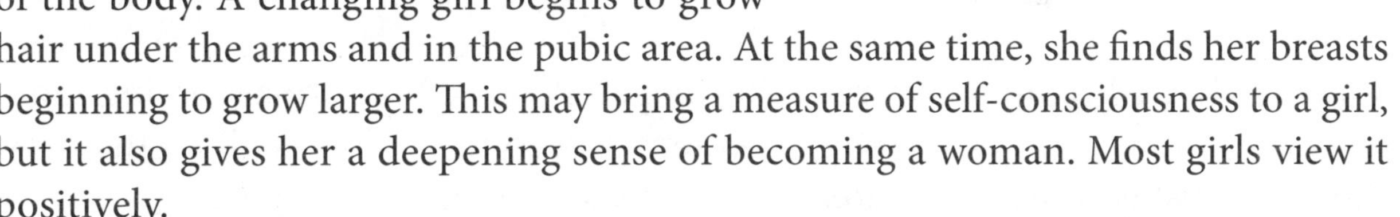

Some girls experience these changes later than others, and some to a lesser degree. Those girls whose breasts change later or not as noticeably need not worry that something is wrong with them.

Two reproductive organs, called ovaries, lie inside the female body toward the lower back side of the abdomen. During the time of female change, these organs begin to develop tiny eggs. Once each month an egg will pass from an ovary down a tube into the womb. The womb is a special organ where babies are formed if the egg is fertilized by male sperm.

God arranged that unfertilized eggs do not stay in the womb, but that each month the womb is flushed by the bloodstream. The blood flows from the womb, down a passageway that opens between the legs. This cleansing, called the menstrual flow or period, lasts approximately five days.

During a woman's period, she needs to wear something to absorb the blood flow. Girls need to be told about these changes in their bodies before they occur, or they will surely be anxious about what may be wrong with them. The monthly period, however, is perfectly normal. In some periods, the blood flow is greater, and some cramping may occur. This is to be expected and should create no fears. Sometimes, however, it is advisable not to be strenuously active in the first days of the period when the flow is heaviest.

A girl who has questions about this part of womanhood should discuss them openly with her mother or with a trusted Christian woman.

Discuss these questions with your parents.

5. Have you experienced any physical changes yet?

6. As a girl, what should you do if your first period starts when you are away from home?

7. As a girl, are there any habits or actions you will need to change or become more careful with in growing up?

A Special Warning

When girls are becoming women, they begin to sense they are becoming more attractive to men. It is not wrong to be attractive to men. God made us that way. But girls must become more careful how they act and talk and appear.

Some girls become silly and begin to flirt with boys and young men. God warns against women acting this way.

> *"Because the daughters of Zion are haughty, and walk with stretched forth necks and wanton eyes, walking and mincing as they go, and making a tinkling with their feet: therefore the Lord will smite with a scab the crown of the head of the daughters of Zion" (Isaiah 3:16, 17).*

In the New Testament, God instructs women to "adorn themselves in modest apparel, with shamefacedness and sobriety" (1 Timothy 2:9). The word translated *shamefacedness* has the idea of modesty and even bashfulness toward men. There is a proper friendliness girls may have toward both men and women, but there is also a reserve around men that is proper. This reserve helps to protect women from carnal and ungodly men.

Most girls do not like to see other girls flirt. They think it looks foolish. It does. Some girls, however, may not realize they are flirting, but think their actions are a normal part of growing up. Here are a few characteristics of flirting. As you discuss these with your parents, perhaps you can think of more.

» Being loud and giggly around boys

» Teasing or slapping boys

» Winking, rolling the eyes, or gesturing in ways to attract boys

» Walking or sitting in ways that show off

» Flattering boys

» ______________________________

» ______________________________

» ______________________________

A Prayer for Girls

Dear God,

Thank You for making me a girl. Thank You for the plans You have for changing my body as I become a woman. I know that what You do is good. You are a marvelous Creator. As I grow up, help me to have a beautiful heart that pleases You. Keep me from trying to attract boys and men with artificial beauty or wrong conduct. Thank You for my mother and for all the examples in the Bible of godly women. Help me to be like them. Amen.

(Signed) ____________________

Why God Made Male and Female

Lesson 5

A Strong Unit

> *"The Lord God said, It is not good that the man should be alone; I will make him an help meet for him. Therefore shall a man leave his father and his mother, and shall cleave unto his wife: and they shall be one flesh" (Genesis 2:18, 24).*

When God made man, He said man was not complete—man needed someone to help him. God created a woman, then, to meet man's incompleteness. Just as man has needs a woman can meet, so a woman has needs a man can meet. Meeting one another's needs is one of the blessings of marriage.

There are other purposes of marriage as well. Marriage can provide for security, friendship, understanding, wisdom, strength, and refinement of character. It is a practical way of combining skills to provide for food, clothes, and shelter.

God made male and female so that they could bear children. It takes a man and a woman together to have a child. Again, the things discussed in this lesson are right and good. They are part of God's plan. But they are things to discuss with parents, not to make light of or to talk about in coarse, dirty ways.

Complete this activity with your parents.

1. Make a list of purposes for God making male and female. (As parents, you may wish to list ways in which each makes the other complete.)

______________________	______________________
______________________	______________________
______________________	______________________
______________________	______________________
______________________	______________________

Reproduction

"Adam knew Eve his wife; and she conceived, and bare Cain, and said, I have gotten a man from the Lord*" (Genesis 4:1).*

In the last two lessons, you learned that God made women so that each month an egg is formed and travels down a special tube into the womb. You also learned God made men so that their reproductive glands produce sperm—tiny "seeds" stored in semen.

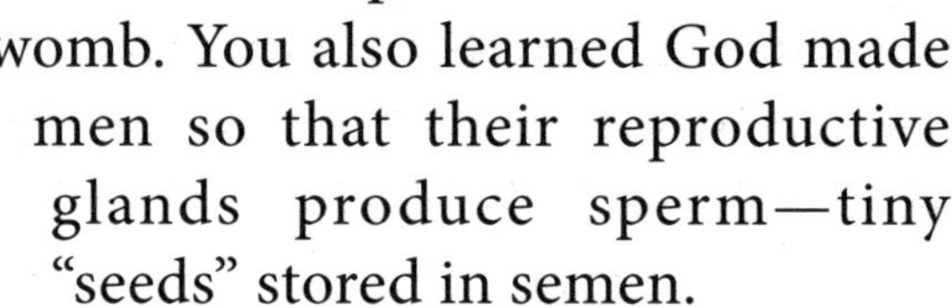

For a woman to have a baby, the egg in her womb needs to be united with a sperm from a man. This happens in a special union between a husband and his wife. In Genesis 4:1 this union is described as "Adam knew Eve." That is a good way to describe it. The physical union between a husband and a wife is a very private and a very intimate union. It is a special act of love.

Today we call this act of love sexual intercourse. In intercourse, the sperm from the husband's reproductive glands travel through an opening in the wife called the vagina. The vagina leads to the womb.

Again, this is a very private and intimate union. A husband and wife have intercourse not only to have babies, but to express their love and commitment to each other. Only at certain times of the month does a wife have an egg that can be fertilized. If a husband and wife come together physically at other times of the month, the wife will not have a baby. God planned that the physical union of a husband and wife should be very pleasurable. In marriage, sexual intercourse is right and good—one of the most special and beautiful things a husband and wife can experience together. Outside of marriage, however, it is cheap and sinful.

When a sperm and egg unite, they form what is called a zygote. It is very tiny, but God designed the zygote to grow rapidly. It is then called an embryo until it is about two months old. By that time, most of the organs are formed, and it is called a fetus. About nine months after this whole process begins, a new baby is born. The changes that take place from the tiny egg-sperm union until birth are phenomenal. Only God could design such living wonders.

A Christian husband and wife look at their children with great joy. Each one is a product of their love and God's creative work. Having children is one of the highest privileges of marriage. It also becomes a tremendous responsibility as Christian parents nurture their children for God.

Look at each verse with your parents and discuss the idea suggested.

2. Psalm 139:13-16 — God knew all about you even while you were forming in your mother's womb.

3. Psalm 127:3 — Children are a blessing from God.

4. Genesis 4:25 — Every child is born through the physical union of a man and woman.

5. Ephesians 5:3-6 — Marriage is the only right place for sexual intercourse. In marriage it is an act of love and commitment that God blesses, but outside of marriage it is an act of lust and selfishness that God condemns.

Many people today use shady or vulgar terms to describe private parts of the body or the act of physical union between a husband and wife. There are proper terms to use. Knowing these terms will help you when you discuss these things with your parents. It will help to keep your thoughts and speech clean.

breasts (brests) The female organs that produce milk for babies.

conception (kən sep′ shən) The time an egg becomes fertile, when new life begins. Also **conceive** (kən sēv′).

ejaculation (i ja′ kyə lā′ shən) The release of semen from the male organ or penis.

embryo (em′ brē ō′) An unborn baby, especially in early stages.

fertilize (fər′ tə līz′) To make an egg able to develop by bringing sperm into contact with it.

fetus (fē′ təs) An unborn baby, especially in later stages.

fornication (for′ nə kā′ shən) The sin of having intercourse before marriage.

intercourse (in′ tər kȯrs′) Physical union between a male and female. Also called **coitus** (kō′ ə təs) or **copulation** (kä′ pyə lā′ shən).

menstruation (men′ strü wā′ shən) The monthly cleansing of a woman's womb. Also called a period.

ovaries (ō′ və rēz) Female organs in the lower abdomen that produce eggs.

penis (pē′ nəs) Male organ between the legs through which semen is ejected.

pregnant (preg′ nənt) Carrying an unborn baby.

puberty (pyü′ bər tē) The time when sexual changes take place in a boy or girl.

pubic (pyü′ bik) Relating to the area from the lower abdomen to the upper thighs.

semen (sē′ mən) The fluid in which sperm is stored in the male.

sperm (spərm) The "seed" that unites with an egg at conception—the sperm "determines" whether the new baby will be male or female.

testicles (te′ sti kəlz) The male reproductive organs located in a sac behind the penis. Also called **genitals** (je′ nə təlz); *genitals* is a term that includes all exterior reproductive organs.

vagina (və jī′ nə) The female tract leading to the womb that receives the penis in intercourse and through which the flow occurs in menstruation.

womb (wüm) The female organ in which babies form. Also called **uterus** (yü′ tə rəs).

Sometimes young people think about private parts of their bodies or about intercourse. Some like to think about this most of the time, and others feel guilty if they think about it at all. A good way to keep your thoughts healthy is to talk these things over with your parents or perhaps with a minister or a minister's wife.

It is not wrong to think about these things. God made our bodies. He planned for male and female and for reproduction. Certainly, we can think too much about our bodies. But when boys' and girls' bodies are changing, they usually become very aware of themselves and of the opposite sex. Part of having healthy thoughts is *how* we think. Learn to thank God for your body. Train your mind to think of other things as well. And again, if you have trouble, talk to your parents. God gave you parents to help you through these times.

Discuss with your parents how these verses apply to you. Write down at least one good idea from your discussion of each verse.

6. Philippians 4:8 ______________________________

7. Matthew 5:27-30 ______________________________

8. James 1:12-15 ______________________________

Prayer

Dear God,

Thank You for making male and female. I know this is part of Your good plan for mankind. Help me never to talk foolishly about the physical relationship between a husband and wife. Most of all, help me to keep my body pure so that if You bless me with a (husband, wife), I can enjoy Your blessing on our marriage union. Thank You for my parents and for the gift of life You gave me through them. Help us to work together in my growing-up years. Amen.

(Signed) ____________________

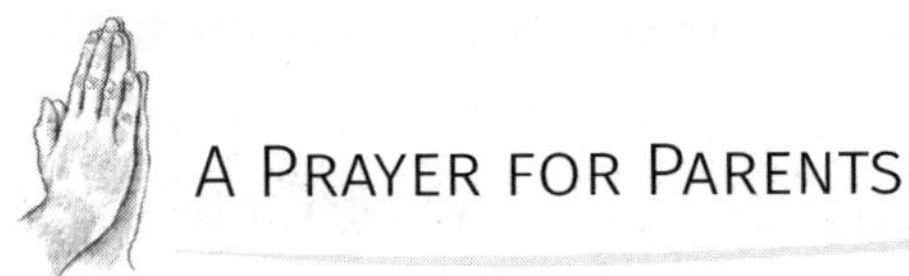

A Prayer for Parents

Dear God,

Thank You for ____________________. (He, She) is the product of our love and Your creative design. As ____________________ grows, please help (him, her) to become the (man, woman) You want (him, her) to be. We commit ourselves to doing our part in teaching, training, and living as good examples. Please be our wisdom and strength in this great responsibility. Amen.

(Father) ____________________ (Mother) ____________________

How I Feel About My Body

Lesson 6

Caution—Construction Area!

Have you ever watched when a small road is turned into a superhighway? It is quite a process. Familiar signs and turns disappear. The whole area is torn up, and the road is bumpy for a while. Caution signs warn travelers to go easy until the new part is finished.

Growing up is a little like that. You are changing from a child into an adult, and sometimes you may feel as though everything familiar has been torn up. There may be some bumpy traveling for a while. This lesson will help you understand yourself. A few caution signs will be raised to help you avoid some of the bumps and hurts of adolescence.

> *"They measuring themselves by themselves, and comparing themselves among themselves, are not wise" (2 Corinthians 10:12).*

Most adolescents hit some bumps of inferiority. Many times it has to do with some physical characteristic. They feel their ears are too big, their hair is too straight, their nose is too long, or that they are too short, tall, fat, or skinny. Other times it has to do with ability. They feel they can't play ball well, can't sing, can't visit naturally, can't get good grades, can't do anything really well.

Inferiority makes us feel bad. We may be shy, or we may be loud, but underneath we keep wondering, *How do others feel about me?*

The worst thing about inferiority, though, is what it can lead to. Sometimes when people feel inferior, they try to cover up their feelings by showing off or being irritable or bossy or loud. They may spend much time and money on their appearance to try to cover blemishes and make themselves attractive. Worse yet, they may begin to point out and laugh at peculiarities or faults in others. This is a cheap way of trying to keep the attention off their own faults.

In many ways, inferiority is a process of comparing ourselves with others. Because we always find someone better, we never quite seem to measure up. So we live in the continued misery of fear and insecurity.

What is the way out of inferiority?

We do not overcome inferiority merely by trying not to compare ourselves with others. The root problem is not so much in our view of others as our view of ourselves. Inferiority often comes back to something about ourselves we resent or are ashamed of. The first step in overcoming inferiority, then, is learning to accept ourselves for who we are.

God made you. He either arranged for or allowed all the things that have made you who you are today. Some things in your life you cannot change. Your height, your hair, your ears, your family, your intelligence, your basic personality—all these are things you do not control. The best thing you can do is accept them. This is *you.*

There are other things about you that can be changed. Your manners, your skills, the care of your body, your attitudes, your speech—these are things you can develop in either good ways or poor ways. The best thing you can do about these things is to seek to please God in them. *When we seek God's approval, the approval of others does not need to control us.*

The second step out of inferiority is to accept others for who they are. When we laugh at others or are critical of them, we are actually hurting ourselves. Others will more easily laugh at us. One common way of making fun is to use nicknames that call attention to a person's odd characteristics—"Long-Ears," "Fatty," "Dummy," etc. On the other hand, when we accept others, when we overlook their faults, when we show kindness and consideration, others are not as likely to look down on us.

Complete these activities.

1. List some of the ways you have felt inferior.

____

____

____

2. List some of the things inferiority leads to.

____

____

____

3. What are two important steps in overcoming inferiority?

a. ______________________________

b. ______________________________

4. Read Leviticus 19:14. Discuss with your parents what this verse means. Then make the commitment.

When I see someone with odd physical features or with physical handicaps, I purpose NOT to make fun of that person. I will not use nicknames that hurt others. I purpose to accept others and to show kindness and consideration, just as I would want to be treated if I were in the same shoes.

(Signed) ______________________

Caution—Peer Pressure!

"Thou shalt not follow a multitude to do evil" (Exodus 23:2).

Peer pressure is closely related to inferiority. The two problems are like two bumps in a row. When we hit one, we usually hit the other also. Young people have a tremendous desire for approval from their friends. To wear a dress or a shirt that doesn't meet the approval of friends or to have a haircut different from the other boys or not to have a vest or jacket like the other girls—any of these can be upsetting to a young person. *What will my friends think?* is a repeated question.

Peer pressure can have its good side. A group of well-behaved boys can cause a troublemaker to watch his behavior. A group of modest, discreet girls can cause a flirt to simmer down.

Many times, however, peer pressure works the other way, especially in a setting where there is not much respect for authority. A group of rebellious young people may try any number of wrong things. There is tremendous pressure to conform in such a group setting. For one boy or one girl to say, "I won't do that," takes a lot of courage.

What kind of negative peer pressure might you face? Make a list of things you might be pressured to do that you know would be wrong. Discuss with your parents what would be possible responses to these pressures.

» ______________________________

» ______________________________

» ______________________________

Caution—Independence!

"Be not wise in thine own eyes" (Proverbs 3:7).

Part of growing up is learning to do things on your own. Your mother and father will not always be around to tell you what to wear, to remind you of work to be done, or to show you how to do something. As you grow into adulthood, you will be much more responsible for deciding, planning, working, buying, and suchlike things. We call this independence.

Of course, no one is fully independent. Adults continue to depend on others, including their parents. But they are responsible for themselves in ways they were not as children.

Adolescents usually look forward to more independence. They often ask for privileges before they are ready. An eight-year-old, for example, may beg to drive the car or pickup. Would you like to ride with an eight-year-old driver?

Parents' responsibility is to train their children to handle decisions and tasks. There usually is a certain amount of conflict between adolescents wanting more independence and parents needing to train and give guidance.

This area of growing up can become very bumpy. The following pointers can help both you and your parents.

» Young people need to respect their parents; parents need to be considerate of young people.

» Talk about your differences rather than argue.

» Where there are privileges, there needs to be accountability.

» Spend time doing things together.

Complete these activities.

5. Have you had conflict with your parents about decisions or activities you felt you were ready for, but they didn't? List them.

______________________ ______________________

______________________ ______________________

______________________ ______________________

6. What kinds of conflicts do many teens have with their parents?

____

____

____

____

7. List some ways you need your parents.

____

____

____

____

8. Read these verses with your parents and discuss how they apply: Deuteronomy 27:16; Proverbs 20:11; 23:24; 28:7.

So many things about you change in the process of becoming an adult. Your body changes. Your thinking changes. Your values change. (Who your age cares about dolls and coloring books?) As you change, you sometimes feel inferior. You want to be accepted by your friends. You want to do challenging things like older people.

During these changes, *you need your parents.* Read the following commitments. Discuss them with your parents. Then sign them and pray together that God will help you to carry them out in the coming years.

Dear Mom and Dad,

In the years ahead, I know I will sometimes disagree with you. But I also know I need you. I want to respect you. Where you must be firm with me, please be firm. Where you can trust me, please do. And please be patient with me. I want to be able to talk with you about my problems and learn from you how to make wise decisions and live a life pleasing to God. I commit myself to honoring you as my parents. Thank you for caring about me the way you do.

(Signed) ____________________

Dear ____________________,

In the years ahead, we know we will sometimes disagree with you. We probably will make some mistakes. But we love you. We want to be considerate of you as a person with needs and thoughts and feelings of your own. We are committed to talking with you, listening to you, and giving the guidance God expects Christian parents to give. Thank you for loving us.

(Father) ____________________ (Mother) ____________________

Keeping My Body Pure

Lesson 7

God Wants Me to Be Pure

"For this is the will of God, even your sanctification, that ye should abstain from fornication: that every one of you should know how to possess his vessel in sanctification and honour; not in the lust of concupiscence, even as the Gentiles which know not God . . . for God hath not called us unto uncleanness, but unto holiness" (1 Thessalonians 4:3-7).

God created your body. All that He does is good. All the parts of your body are pure and right as God created them. It is only as we use our bodies in wrong ways that they become impure. Everyone faces temptations to do impure things, but not everyone yields to these temptations. This lesson is about how to overcome temptation and keep your body pure.

The verses above use several words you may not be familiar with. *Sanctification* means "holy." In these verses, it especially refers to being pure in our bodies. *Fornication* means "having intercourse before marriage." And *concupiscence* means "evil or perverted desires." These kinds of desires come especially through using our sex organs wrongly.

God makes it very clear that intercourse is for marriage. In marriage, it is beautiful and right. But outside of marriage, it is selfish and sinful. As you grow and develop sexually, you will find that your body has strong urges. You will want to think about the opposite sex. This is normal, but you must learn to control these urges and thoughts.

Sometimes you will probably wonder why God allowed young men and women to have such strong desires before they are emotionally mature enough for the responsibilities of marriage. The years between puberty and marriage, however, are important years. They provide opportunity and time to develop self-control and emotional and spiritual strength. Everyone needs these qualities in marriage. Getting married does not mean a man and woman can do as they please sexually. They must be considerate and caring of one another, and for this to be possible, they must be in control of their sexual desires.

In our day, many sinful people are having intercourse before marriage. The results of this looseness are terrible. Many unmarried teenage girls become pregnant each year, and their children are born without having a proper home.

Some people today try to "correct" these teenage pregnancies by recommending abortion. They think it is better to kill the baby than to burden the teenager with its care. This is only adding sin to sin. Abortion is horrible. Although the baby may be tiny, it is alive. Killing it only adds to the guilt of the parents.

Another result of disobeying God in this is what is called venereal disease. People who have intercourse with more than one partner easily contract and transmit venereal diseases. Among young people today, venereal diseases are widespread. These young people are reaping for not obeying God (Galatians 6:8).

Some young people struggle with what is called masturbation. This is using one's own hands to rub the sex organs to produce a pleasurable feeling. The Bible does not specifically talk about this. It does warn, however, against thinking lustful thoughts. Lustful thoughts always accompany masturbation. Also, when masturbation becomes a repeated practice, it seems to make sex desires stronger. God wants us to control these desires. Masturbation goes against God's instruction, "Keep thyself pure" (1 Timothy 5:22). God wants us to keep our bodies pure so that if we marry, our marriage and home will be healthy and strong. And if we do not marry, He wants us to be pure so that He can fill us with His Holy Spirit and use us in His work.

Fill in the blanks.

1. God wants us to be ________________.

2. Outside of ________________, intercourse is selfish and sinful.

3. God can help you ________________ the strong urges that may cause you to think about having intercourse.

4. When people have intercourse before marriage, ________________ are born without having a proper ________________.

5. When people have intercourse with more than one partner, they may contract ________________ ________________.

6. Masturbation is accompanied with ________________ ________________, which are sinful.

Overcoming Temptation

Knowing that God wants you to be pure is encouraging. This means He will be with you in times of temptation. "God is our refuge and strength, a very present help in trouble" (Psalm 46:1). "There hath no temptation taken you but such as is common to man: **but God is faithful,** who will not suffer you to be tempted above that ye are able; but will with the temptation also make a way to escape, that ye may be able to bear it" (1 Corinthians 10:13).

Here are several pointers for overcoming temptation. You may go over these with your parents now. And in time to come, you may wish to review these pointers for encouragement and help.

1. **Honor your parents.** You may not understand this, but there seems to be a direct tie between rebellion and immorality. Those who resist their parents simply cannot seem to resist temptation. A Biblical example of this would be Eli's sons (see 1 Samuel 2:12-25).
2. **Fill your mind with good things.** We cannot keep out every wrong thought, but we can accustom our minds to right thinking. Read good books. Develop a practice of reading from the Bible each day. Especially if you have become ensnared in immoral thoughts or habits, use the Bible to cleanse your mind. "Wherewithal shall a young man cleanse his way? by taking heed thereto according to thy word" (Psalm 119:9). Memorize verses you find especially helpful, or paraphrase them, writing them out in your own words with your name.

3. **Avoid sources of temptation.** The Bible often encourages us to stand against temptation. We are told to "flee" immoral situations. "Flee fornication" (1 Corinthians 6:18). "Flee also youthful lusts" (2 Timothy 2:22). Joseph "left his garment in her hand, and fled, and got him out" (Genesis 39:12). If a place or a person or a situation presents you with temptation, GET AWAY from that place or person or situation.

4. **Never follow your curiosity into what you know is immoral.** One of the biggest traps of Satan in this area is immoral literature. Like Job, we need to make a "covenant with [our] eyes" (Job 31:1) to avoid looking at what would tempt us. Another trap of Satan in this area is curiosity about our own body. God made us, and our bodies are not evil. But we must treat private areas of our body with respect. Curiosity leads easily to masturbation. Sometimes we are tempted to think, *If I try something, maybe I won't have so much trouble thinking about it.* That is false. Involvement in immoral thoughts, pictures, movies, or actions always leads us away from purity, never toward it. Impure thoughts and actions easily become hard-to-break habits. When you are tempted to follow your curiosity about immorality, instead follow Proverbs 4:15. "Avoid it, pass not by it, turn from it, and pass away."

5. **Have good friends.** Friends are important to young people. Being accepted is important to young people. But having good friends is more important than having popular friends. The Bible warns, "Be not deceived: evil communications corrupt good manners" (1 Corinthians 15:33). The simple meaning of that verse is that bad company will corrupt our morals.

6. **Work hard.** This may sound like an unrelated suggestion. But hard work is morally beneficial in several ways. First, just needing to concentrate is good for our minds. Second, work can help to relieve sexual urges—the body channels its energies into the work at hand. Third, hard work is good discipline and thus strengthens character.

7. **Keep clean and neat in your appearance, but avoid decoration and immodesty.** What we see affects us. But how we appear to others affects both them and us. The Bible teaches modesty simply because immodesty invites sin. Both God and good people admire Christian character. Let God's approval be your goal.

8. **Fear the Lord.** The fear of the Lord enables us to "depart from evil" (Proverbs 3:7). Joseph showed this. When Potiphar's wife tempted him, saying, "Lie with me," Joseph responded, "How then can I do this great wickedness, and sin against God?" (Genesis 39:7, 9). We develop a healthy fear of God by reading and obeying His Word.

9. **If you have become ensnared in thoughts or habits you cannot seem to overcome, confide in a mature Christian.** Talk to your parents or minister about your problem. Make yourself accountable to them. For example, ask them to ask you periodically how you are doing. Be honest. Pray together. They can help you to find in Christ the strength to live victoriously.

Complete these activities with your parents.

7. Which of these suggestions do you think is most important for you? (Write it and discuss why it is important.) ____________________

____

____

8. List some possible sources of temptation for you. Then discuss how to avoid them.

____________	____________
____________	____________
____________	____________

9. Psalm 51 is a prayer of David after he had committed adultery with Bathsheba. It shows how guilty one feels after such a sin. It also shows how to find forgiveness when one has sinned. Read this psalm with your parents. Write several thoughts that impress you.

____

____

____

PRAYER

Dear God,

Thank You for making male and female and for the attractions we have for each other. Thank You also for the clear teaching in the Bible on how we should control our desires. I want You to know I desire to live a pure life. Please help me to be wise. I purpose to avoid sources of temptation, including all books, magazines, pictures, music, and people that would draw my mind into lustful thoughts. Thank You that You want me to be pure and that You will help me. Amen.

(Signed) ____________________

Caring for My Body

Lesson 8

Why I Should Care for My Body

"Thus saith the Lord that made thee, and formed thee from the womb, which will help thee" (Isaiah 44:2).

Why should you take care of your body? First, because God made it. If you received a shiny new bike as a gift, you would probably want to take care of it, right? You wouldn't leave it out in the rain to weather and rust. If it needed cleaning, you would clean it. If it needed oiling, you would oil it. If it needed care of any sort, you would want to give it. Your care of the gift would show your respect to the one who gave it.

Even so, caring for your body shows respect for the One who made it and gave it to you. God is pleased when we take good care of our bodies.

"What? know ye not that your body is the temple of the Holy Ghost which is in you, which ye have of God, and ye are not your own? For ye are bought with a price: therefore glorify God in your body, and in your spirit, which are God's" (1 Corinthians 6:19, 20).

A second reason you should care for your body is because God wants to live in you by His Spirit. A Christian can look at his body as God's "temple." When God lives in us, our hands, our feet, our tongue—all the members of our body—are to be under God's direction.

When this is so, we will be careful not to knowingly do anything that would damage our bodies. For this reason, Christians avoid foods and drink they know can cause disease or damage to them. "Whether therefore ye eat, or drink, or whatsoever ye do, do all to the glory of God" (1 Corinthians 10:31).

Discuss each of the following items with your parents. List the ways these things can damage people's health. Then discuss how you might be pressured or tempted to try these things and what your response should be.

Tobacco	
Damage	
Temptations	
Response	

Strong Drink	
Damage	
Temptations	
Response	

Mind-Altering Drugs	
Damage	
Temptations	
Response	

There would be no one hooked on tobacco, alcohol, or drugs if everyone would say NO the first time.

How I Should Care for My Body

During adolescence, many physical changes are taking place. Physical growth, mental and emotional development, as well as youthful activities all consume a lot of energy. These suggestions give practical ways you can experience these changes healthily.

1. **Get plenty of rest.** Most adolescents need eight to ten hours of rest each night. People vary, of course. But much as you may wish to stay up late at night, good rest is necessary for you.
2. **Get plenty of exercise.** Exercise can come both in work and in play. But God made our muscles and bones so that use is healthy, and disuse is not. Do your chores with gusto. It is not only a good way to get them done, but it helps you to feel better. Good rest often is dependent on good exercise.
3. **Eat good food.** Many adolescents like "junk food." But growing bodies need food rich in vitamins, minerals, and protein. This does not mean you should never eat chips or drink pop, but that you should eat a good balance of grains, meats, vegetables, and milk products.
4. **Keep yourself clean and neat.** The way you think about yourself depends a lot on how you care for yourself. Regularly brush your teeth, comb your hair, wash your hands, trim your nails, use deodorant, and dress appropriately. You will work better, play better, feel better, and grow better. Of course, you can overdo these things, but personal hygiene is basic to a good attitude.

Evaluate your health habits.

1. a. How much sleep do I average per night? ________________

b. Am I often tired? ________________

2. a. Do I get good exercise daily? ________________

b. What kinds of exercise do I enjoy? ________________________________

____

c. Are there ways I could get more or better exercise? ____________________

____

3. a. Do I enjoy food from each of the four food groups? ______________________

   b. What healthful foods do I not enjoy? ______________________

   ____

   c. How might I learn to like them? ______________________

   ____

   d. Are there particular foods with little nutritional value that I eat too much (or would like to)? ______________________

   ____

4. In each of the following matters of personal grooming, do I do okay, or do I need improvement?

   a. brushing teeth ______________ d. bathing ______________

   b. hair care ______________ e. deodorant ______________

   c. manicure ______________ f. appropriate dress ______________

5. After evaluating your health habits, discuss this with your parents. Do they agree with your evaluation? If necessary, make a list of some things you need to improve.

   ____

   ____

   ____

   ____

6. Explain what changes you are willing to make to develop good health habits.

   ____

   ____

   ____

PRAYER

Dear God,

Thank You for giving me my body. I know everything You make is good. I also know You want to live in me, and I want to care for my body so it can be a temple for You. Help me to have the courage to say no when I face pressure to do things that would damage my body. Please be with me during my growing-up years, so that I can honor You with my body and be a good example for others. Amen.

(Signed) ______________________

Contemporary Issues: Gender Confusion

Lesson 9

Note to students: As each generation in our society knows less and less about God and His will, society seems to go further and further from God. People live more selfishly and sinfully. This leads to sins becoming common that were not common in the past. It is good for godly parents and their young people to discuss these kinds of issues. The last lessons of the workbook deal with two of them: gender confusion and the use of technology.

Make sure your parents have looked at this part of the workbook before you begin, because they may want to discuss parts of it with you and give you some directions before you start.

Gender Confusion

> *"God saw every thing that he had made, and, behold, it was very good" (Genesis 1:31).*

God made us male and female. This is good. Girls look forward to becoming women, boys to becoming men. Our bodies are different, but that is not all. Women enjoy mothering and doing household tasks, and men like mechanical things and work that calls for strength.

But sometimes girls prefer doing things boys do or vice versa. Even adults sometimes enjoy activities that are more commonly done by the opposite gender. Men may enjoy cooking or even specialize in a skill like sewing. And some ladies love to do fieldwork. It isn't wrong to enjoy an activity that normally is done by the opposite gender.

Still, God created men and women to be different. Men have a hormone called testosterone that makes them physically and mentally different. Men are usually more aggressive and physically competitive. They often measure themselves by what they can get done. Women, on the other hand, tend to measure themselves by relationships. They are drawn to special events and appealing atmospheres. However, a woman may enjoy physical competition, or a man may care about having a nice atmosphere in a restaurant.

God made men and women with these differences for specific purposes. Some people think boys and girls learn differences only by being raised that way and by watching their parents and others around them. But that is not true; the differences are "programmed into us"—God specifically designed us that way.

The Bible teaches differing roles for men and women. God calls husbands to lead their families with self-sacrificing love. He calls wives to support their husbands and to be good homemakers. In the church, God calls men to lead and women to support.

Serious problems arise when people reject God's intentions for men and women. Many today do not follow God or honor His ways. We will look at two significant problems of today.

Homosexuality

"Know ye not that the unrighteous shall not inherit the kingdom of God? Be not deceived: neither fornicators, nor idolaters, nor adulterers, nor effeminate, nor abusers of themselves with mankind . . . shall inherit the kingdom of God" (1 Corinthians 6:9, 10).

Sexual attraction for the same gender is called *homosexuality*. Boys often have close boy friendships and girls have close girl friendships. This is normal. But when men are attracted to men in a sexual way or when women are attracted to women in that way, it is not normal. To engage in sexual activity with someone of the same gender is against nature and against God's plan.

Usually, not many people have these same-sex attractions. But when people focus on getting all the sexual pleasure they can in any way they please, strange and unnatural attractions can increase. In our society, many people believe it is okay to pursue whatever sexual urges they feel. However, God says homosexual activity is sin; it is a sexual desire that is twisted, unnatural, and turned to a wrong use.

Although it is rare, boys and girls who grow up in Christian homes may sometimes feel these desires. We don't always know why this is. Some influence or event in the young person's life may have affected his or her normal sexual desire. Some who experience these desires say they have had them as long as they can remember. It is not so important to know *why* a person has an unnatural desire; but it *is* important to honor God's directions. God designed the male body to fit the female body, and this is the only proper way to have sexual relations.

Read each Scripture and complete the sentences.

1. Leviticus 18:22. God views sexual relations between a man and another man as an ________________.

2. Leviticus 20:13. The penalty in the Old Testament for homosexual behavior was ________________.

Read Romans 1:26, 27. Fill in the blanks.

3. Here Paul is describing a culture that departs from God and rejects His ways.
   a. "God gave them up unto ________________ affections: for even their women did change the ________________ use into that which is against ________________."
   b. "Likewise also the men, leaving the ________________ use of the woman, burned in their lust one toward another; men with men working that which is ________________, and receiving in themselves that recompence of their error which was meet."

> *"In the day that God created man, in the likeness of God made he him; male and female created he them; and blessed them, and called their name Adam, in the day when they were created"* (Genesis 5:1, 2).

Another growing gender problem in our society is that of a boy thinking of himself as being a female or a girl thinking of herself as being a male. These people are typically referred to as being transgender.

A boy with this unnatural desire may prefer visiting with girls and ladies rather than with his male acquaintances. He may "want to be a girl," and try to act and talk like a girl or try to do things that girls or ladies typically do. He may resist doing things boys normally do. A girl, on the other hand, may want to be a man instead of being a woman. She may try to talk and act like a man, do things men normally do, and resent that her body looks female rather than male.

It is fine for girls to enjoy things that boys do or for men to enjoy activities that women commonly do, like cooking or sewing. Transgender desires, however, are much stronger than that. They involve wanting to identify completely as the opposite gender.

We do not always know why a person has these feelings or desires, but those with such desires must choose to honor God's design. A male needs to accept being a male, even if he thinks he would prefer to be a female. Acting, dressing, or talking like a female is resisting the way God made him. It creates confusion. The same is true for a person with a female body who thinks she wants to be a male.

Sometimes transgender desires are mixed with homosexuality.

The Scriptures do not use the term *transgender*. Both the Old and New Testaments teach that the genders are to be kept distinct. Furthermore, God made us, and to resist the way He made us is to dishonor Him.

Read these verses and answer the questions.

4. Genesis 1:27. Who thought up the idea of two genders? ____________________

5. Genesis 1:31. What did God say about all that He had made? ____________________

____

6. Deuteronomy 22:5
   a. How are the genders to be distinguished according to this law?

   ____

   b. In the Old Testament, how did God view men and women confusing their identity by wearing clothing of the opposite gender?

   ____

7. Psalm 139:13-16
   a. How does David describe his formation before he was born?

   ____

   b. The *Amplified Bible* puts verse 15 this way: "My frame was not hidden from You when I was being formed in secret [and] intricately and curiously wrought [as if embroidered with various colors] in the depths of the earth [a region of darkness and mystery]." What additional ideas do you get from this about how you were designed? ______________________________

   ____

   c. What attitude does David have toward his Creator? ______________________________

   ____

8. 1 Corinthians 6:9-11
   a. What sins are named here that relate to sexual confusion?

   ____

   b. Paul says those who practice these sins will not inherit the ______________.
   c. Paul indicates that some of the Corinthians used to practice these sins. How did they change? ______________________________

   ____

Responses

As we noted earlier, even someone who grows up in a Christian home may sometimes have confusing sexual thoughts and desires. He or she may have been introduced to sexual perversions at an early age. Or sexual confusion may come from friends enticing the youngster to take part in sexual activities. Sometimes, a person might have same-gender attractions and not know why.

When children in Christian homes have same-gender attractions, they typically feel confused and ashamed. They may feel guilty and be afraid to talk to anyone about their feelings. For such young people, it is usually best to talk to a parent or another trusted adult. A godly adult of the same gender can help a young person cope with his fears and learn how to respond to these feelings.

However, talking to an adult could make the problem worse if the adult scolds or shames the young person seeking help. Instead, the adult should listen carefully, be understanding and kind, and offer helpful guidance. If you talk to someone and do not find it helpful, don't be discouraged. You may need to find another godly person who will be more helpful.

Sexual desires are very strong. God created us that way to help us have strong marriages and families. Wrong sexual desires are also very strong. Yielding to them only makes them stronger. The more a person yields to wrong desires, the easier it becomes to sin, and the more natural it seems. Many people who follow their perverted desires have become deceived and claim it is "natural" for them. It takes determination, courage, and strength to follow God, especially since our world encourages us to just do whatever feels right to us.

Following our own desires makes a mess of our lives. If you observe people who freely follow their sexual desires, you will find people who suffer much trouble and heartache, including wasted lives, broken families, hurting children, and sexual diseases. Some of the saddest stories in the Bible are about people who followed their sexual desires against God's directions. They tell of terrible experiences like rape, unfaithfulness, homosexuality, broken families, violence, and death. Following God's directions for our sexuality protects us from many snares and troubles.

The sorrows that come with a life of sexual sins may not become evident until years later. Older people more easily see these consequences. Many of the Proverbs come from an older father who warns his young son about the dangers of sexual sins.

> *"My son, attend unto my wisdom, and bow thine ear to my understanding: that thou mayest regard discretion, and that thy lips may keep knowledge. For the lips of a strange woman drop as an honeycomb, and her mouth is smoother than oil: but her end is bitter as wormwood, sharp as a twoedged sword. Her feet go down to death; her steps take hold on hell" (Proverbs 5:1-5).*

Read these proverbs. Answer one question and discuss the others with your parents.

9. Proverbs 1:10

a. How should you respond if someone urges you to sin? ____________________

____

b. Discuss with your parent(s) what would be a good response to someone who asks you to commit a sexual sin.

10. Proverbs 7:22, 23. Ask your parent(s) to tell you what sorrows they have seen in the lives of people who ignore God's directions and follow their sexual desires.

Even though you may be happy with your gender and want to do right, you may encounter others with these problems. As a young man, for example, you may encounter another young man who is attracted to men, or who would rather be a woman. Or as a young woman, you might suddenly realize another young woman has a sexual attraction for you.

What should you do in such situations?

We might have a variety of feelings in response—ranging from disgust to curiosity. As Proverbs teaches, we should turn from temptation; never yield to pressure to do wrong. "Enter not into the path of the wicked, and go not in the way of evil men. Avoid it, pass not by it, turn from it" (Proverbs 4:14, 15).

Probably the first thing you should do is to tell a godly older person. If your friend tries to get you to do sinful things, you should avoid being alone with him or her.

Sometimes people (including Christians) respond wrongly to sexually confused people, and that adds to the problem. Here are some harmful and wrong responses:

1. **Teasing.** Don't mock, laugh at, or make jokes about someone's sexual struggles.
2. **Name-calling.** Don't speak unkindly of them or call them names. When men are attracted to men, the proper term is *homosexual* or *gay.* When women are attracted to women, the proper term is *lesbian. Transgender* is the term for a person who wishes he or she were the opposite gender. Follow the Golden Rule; respect them as being created by God.
3. **Bullying.** Sometimes people become the target of unkind actions, pranks, and meanness. We should never treat others unkindly, no matter how different or wrong they are. Some young people have even committed suicide because their peers bullied them so much that they didn't want to live anymore.

4. **Condemnation.** Don't tell a person God hates them or that they are terrible. It is true that any sexual relationship outside of marriage is sinful. God loves all people and wants all of us, whatever our sins, to repent. While we may say certain actions are sinful, we should invite people to turn to God and follow His ways.

   If you know someone who struggles with wrong sexual attractions, you might want to try to help them. But usually a person needs help from an older, mature person. He or she may, without realizing it, draw you into a relationship that is unwise and even harmful. Don't tell them that you will keep secrets. Urge them to get help from a wise and mature Christian.

Read the following verses, discuss them with your parent(s), and tell how they might apply to the way you relate to a person who struggles with homosexuality or transgender desires.

11. Ephesians 4:15 ____________________

12. Ephesians 5:3, 4 ____________________

13. Ephesians 5:11, 12 ____________________

14. 1 Corinthians 13:5 ____________________

15. Philippians 4:6 ____________________

16. 2 Timothy 2:22 ____________________

Contemporary Issues: Technology

Lesson 10

In the last hundred years, technology has changed our world, from transportation to communication to education to economics—every part of our lives has changed. Many of these changes are good, saving us labor, time, and money. Most young people, for example, would much rather run a rototiller than a hoe, or would prefer to use an electric mixer rather than beat eggs or mash potatoes by hand. Along with the blessings, however, come dangers. What can be used for good purposes can also be used for evil purposes.

In this section, we will explore four electronic technologies and think briefly about the blessings and snares they bring.

The Internet

> *"I will set no wicked thing before mine eyes: I hate the work of them that turn aside; it shall not cleave to me" (Psalm 101:3).*

Beginning in 1989, the World Wide Web (now commonly called the Internet) has allowed people to share information via computers. It has drastically changed how people communicate and interact with each other.

The Internet is a way to get information. Using search engines, we can find information about people, products, and services. We can get phone numbers and addresses. We can see maps that show us how to get to those addresses, how many miles it is from our location, and how long it will take to drive there. We can locate products we want to buy, compare prices, order what we want, and know when it will be delivered to our door.

The Internet is also a huge source of information about the past. We can find information about historical events, places, and people without needing to search through libraries and books to find it.

The Internet is a source of current news. We can read about what is going on all around the world almost immediately after events happen.

Complete this activity with your parents.

1. List some ways you or your family have benefited from the Internet, either directly or indirectly.

 ____

 ____

 ____

Snares

Along with these conveniences come many dangers. The Internet is a source of information about sinful lifestyles. It gives access to movies, video clips, chat rooms, dating sites, porn sites, gambling, and much worldly entertainment. Man's most sinful practices are readily available for viewing on the Internet.

Many children and adolescents have been exposed to sinful living in homes where parents allowed Internet access without safeguards. Even in Christian homes with Internet blocking and monitoring safeguards in place, young people have been ensnared by ads or sites that exposed them to the wicked ways of the world.

Through the Internet, people can contact both friends and strangers and share personal information without having in-person interaction. For many people, this encourages boldness to say and do things they would not say and do in person. This has led people into secret and sinful relationships. It also has made it possible for scheming adults to take advantage of children and adolescents and harm them.

If you have used your parents' or a friend's computer or phone to look at something wrong on the Internet, you should confess it to your parents.

Read each passage from Proverbs. Then tell how it would apply to Internet use.

2. Proverbs 1:10 ____

3. Proverbs 5:3-5 ____

4. Proverbs 14:12 ____

"Blessed is the man that walketh not in the counsel of the ungodly, nor standeth in the way of sinners, nor sitteth in the seat of the scornful" (Psalm 1:1).

One way the Internet has changed communication is through social media. Social media allows people to communicate with friends and relatives and even strangers. On social media sites, people can post pictures and video clips and write about what is happening in their lives. Sites like Facebook, Instagram, and Twitter allow people to accumulate a network of "friends" or "followers" who then can interact with each other electronically.

Through social media, families and relatives can stay in touch with each other even though they live in scattered states or even on different continents. Family members who are traveling can keep home folks posted about their travels. Missionaries can stay in touch with supporting friends and churches, offering prayer requests, updates, and emergency news. All these are blessings.

Snares

But there are downsides to social media.

These downsides are serious, partly because of their effects, but also because they are not easily seen as dangerous. We will consider three dangers of social media, although there are more.

1. **Social media provides only a superficial ("on the surface") connection.** Although messages, pictures, and videos are almost instantaneous, the connection—the relationship—is only a partial one. Knowing someone through social media is not the same kind of knowing that occurs when people are with each other in person.

   Many people today are "learning to know" each other (even dating) through social media. The distance, combined with a false feeling of closeness, leads people to share in ways they would not if they were together in person.

   Because people often express their feelings to each other through social media, they can seem to be "real" to each other. In truth, acquaintance through social media is only a small slice of reality, allowing people to share only certain parts of their lives.

2. **Social media is addictive.** Studies have shown that people quickly become addicted to following friends—or celebrities or complete strangers—on

social media. Some people become so involved that they stay on social media regularly until late at night (or even into the morning).

3. **Social media can lead to loneliness and despair.** Put the first two dangers together, and it is easy to understand why social media can lead to loneliness. People who spend a lot of time online often do not have enough real-life interaction with others. This lack of human interaction can lead to anxiety and depression. Studies have linked the increase in suicide to excessive use of social media.

Discuss these questions with your parents.

5. How have you seen social media affecting people's lives?

6. What are some reasons social media is so attractive and addictive?

7. What guidelines does your family and church have for using social media?

8. What do you think are the most serious dangers of using social media?

Electronic Games

"I will behave myself wisely in a perfect way. O when wilt thou come unto me? I will walk within my house with a perfect heart" (Psalm 101:2).

The world of electronics has exploded with entertaining games. Some of these come as handheld devices. Others operate on computers and require the use of the Internet. Many board games of the past have been replaced with electronic versions. We can now play chess, for example, with people around the world or against a computer on different levels of difficulty. Whereas longer ago, word games like crossword puzzles were found only in newspapers or books, now we can play these either by ourselves or against other players online. Some electronic games are educational, but most are designed primarily for entertainment.

Snares

The potential dangers of electronic games are many. They are addicting; someone starts playing and finds it hard to stop. There have even been instances of people gaming themselves to death—usually from a combination of too much adrenalin and too little sleep.

Electronic games are often time-wasters, keeping people from better activities and even from their responsibilities. Workers have been fired for playing games on company time. Men have neglected their families. Some wives call themselves "gamer widows" because their husbands spend so much time gaming.

By wasting hours playing electronic games, young men and women neglect hands-on, real-life activities. Creativity and healthy development call for us to be engaged in the real world, exercising our muscles, solving real problems, planning, building, and making. Building a birdhouse or making up your own cake recipe—even if they turn out to be huge flops—are better for your mind and body than pushing buttons that light up a screen.

The increasing problem of overweight children and adolescents is both a matter of poor diet and a lack of physical activity. Studies show that allowing toddlers to have a lot of screen time has a negative impact on their brain development.

Another serious problem with electronic games is that many are designed around themes of danger or violence. The most popular video games involve intrigue, fighting, shooting, and blowing up enemies. Not only do these activities go directly against the teaching and example of Jesus, they also feed a violent way of thinking. The person who constantly kills or blows up "problem people" in video games may tend to respond more violently to "problem people" in the real world.

Look up these Scriptures and write how you think they apply to electronic games.

9. a. Ephesians 5:15 (*Circumspectly* means "cautious or careful in making decisions.")

____

b. Ephesians 5:16 ______________________________

10. Philippians 4:8 ______________________________

11. Luke 6:27-31 ______________________________

Cell Phones

> *"Whatsoever things are true, whatsoever things are honest, whatsoever things are just, whatsoever things are pure, whatsoever things are lovely, whatsoever things are of good report; if there be any virtue, and if there be any praise, think on these things" (Philippians 4:8).*

Nearly everything that used to be done by computer—plus many other things—can now be done on smartphones. Smartphones allow people to make payments, search for information, track the stars in the night sky, play music, video chat with friends, set reminders, monitor heart rate and blood pressure, take pictures, send and receive e-mails, read books, follow a to-do list, watch a how-to video, study the Bible . . . the list is almost endless.

Even if you do not have a phone, the following paragraphs will help you understand some of the dangers and responsibilities that smartphones bring.

Snares

Smartphones can also be easily and badly abused. Phones are almost always with us. While this appears to increase their convenience, it also means they invade nearly every area of our lives. We can receive texts or phone calls or notifications while we are working, studying, driving, sleeping, playing a game with the family, eating a meal, visiting with friends, or sitting in Sunday school. It has become normal to see people walking down a sidewalk and looking at their phones. Or worse: a group of people sitting at a table or standing in a circle looking at their phones and ignoring the others.

Many states now have laws forbidding texting or talking on a handheld device while driving because distracted driving has become the number one cause of traffic accidents in the United States.

Smartphones may access the Internet and social media and online video games, so all the snares mentioned with the first three technologies in this lesson apply to smartphones also.

Discuss these questions with your parents.

12. At what age is it appropriate for you to have a phone?

13. What guidelines do you follow as a family for the use of phones?

14. If you were ever to have a smartphone, what should guide your selection of phone apps?

15. What are the pros and cons of having a Bible app on one's phone?

16. What are the dangers of learning to know someone primarily through texting or social media?

Christian Light is a nonprofit, conservative Mennonite publishing company providing Christ-centered, Biblical literature including books, Gospel tracts, Sunday school materials, summer Bible school materials, and a full curriculum for Christian day schools and homeschools. Though produced primarily in English, some books, tracts, and school materials are also available in Spanish.

For more information about the ministry of Christian Light or its publications, or for spiritual help, please contact us at:

ADDRESS :: P. O. Box 1212,
Harrisonburg, VA 22803

TELEPHONE :: 540-434-0768

FAX :: 540-433-8896

E-MAIL :: info@christianlight.org

WEBSITE :: www.christianlight.org